KT-440-557

THE
RIBBON
BOOK

THE
RIBBON
* BOOK *

Juliet Bawden

PIATKUS

For my aunt, Neuritza Dart, with love.

Copyright © Juliet Bawden, 1987

First published in 1987 by
Judy Piatkus (Publishers) Ltd, 5 Windmill St, London W1P 1HF

British Library Cataloguing in Publication Data

Bawden, Juliet
  The ribbon book.
  1. Ribbons   2. Handicraft
  I. Title
  746.2'7   TT880

  ISBN 0–86188–569–4

Edited by Susan Fleming
Illustrated and designed by Paul Saunders
Photography by Helen Pask

Phototypeset in Linotron Baskerville by
Phoenix Photosetting, Chatham
Printed and bound in Great Britain at
The Bath Press, Avon

Contents

Working with Ribbons

Ribbons have been used throughout history for personal adornment. They were worn by both the Greeks and Romans, and the latter decorated their temples with festoons of ribbons during festivals.

The most extensive use of ribbons was from the years 1770 to 1790 when they were a feature of hats, baby caps, parasols and ballgowns; collars were festooned with ribbon embroidery, and skirts had row upon row of gathered ribbon.

The eighteenth-century pirate, Captain Teach – better known as Blackbeard – had a beard which grew from high on his cheeks and reached half-way down his chest. When going into action he would plait his beard into a number of tails and tie it with brightly coloured ribbons to scare his enemies!

By 1800, French silk ribbon was being imported into America, and the Indians from the eastern plains and from northern America were bartering tools and furs with the white population in order to obtain it. They used ribbon appliqué to decorate their shirts, moccasins and dresses. And it was during the last quarter of the ninteenth century that the 'ribbon quilt' – the English version of the American 'log cabin' design – appeared; these quilts were made out of ribbons used for trimming hats.

Ribbons have always been a favourite motif with interior designers and craftsmen. They have been used for wallpaper and fabric design, and there are even ribbon plates: these are pretty ceramic plates, often with a picture in the centre, and holes around the edge through which to thread ribbon. During the eighteenth century, Chippendale sometimes used a form of carved decoration called 'ribbon back' on his chairs. The wood is carved to resemble ribbon tied in bows.

This book is full of ideas for using ribbons in imaginative and unusual ways: I explain how to weave, appliqué, embroider, plait, even how to make flowers, bows, toys and presents from ribbon. I hope you enjoy reading it, and that my ideas will trigger off many more of your own.

Ribbon Glossary

This briefly describes the many types of ribbon which come in all colours and many widths, and is followed by some sewing and gathering tips.

Baby Ribbon   Very narrow ribbon, usually pastel coloured satin; used mainly on baby garments and children's clothes. Ideal as a finish on the cuffs of a puff-sleeved baby dress, or to decorate a christening robe.

Belting Ribbon   Stiff grosgrain. As the name suggests, used for making belts or lining the waistbands of skirts.

Cake Ribbon   Designed to go round birthday cakes and Christmas cakes, it is usually made of a stiff single faced satin ribbon with a non-woven edge.

China Ribbon   This kind of ribbon was at its most popular in the mid-nineteenth century. It was approximately 3mm (⅛ inch) wide with a plain woven edge.

Double-Faced   A double-faced ribbon has a finish on both sides. It usually has a woven edge, and is used when both sides of the ribbon will be seen – for example on a sash or a ribbon rose.

Feather-Edge Satin   A satin ribbon with delicate loops down the edges. Offray make this ribbon in 5mm, 10mm, and 15mm widths (³⁄₁₆, ⅜ and ⅝ inch). It can be machine washed or dry cleaned and shrinks less than 2 per cent. It is best used on formal or evening wear.

Grosgrain   A stiff ribbon with a crossways rib, available in plain, dot or stripe; often used for hat bands, or handles on soft fabric bags. It is stiff enough to make shoe bows. Usually made in polyester, it is easy to wash. It comes in various widths.

Jacquard A ribbon with a woven rather than a printed pattern, therefore often quite heavyweight; these ribbons are usually multi-coloured, sometimes with a metal thread running through the design. The designs are occasionally self-coloured. Popular jacquard designs are those with a heart motif, or a single rose bud or alpine flower.

Knitting Ribbon This is particularly soft and is used for knitting or crochet work. It comes in a matt or a shiny finish, sometimes used on its own or in conjunction with wool or cotton yarn.

Love Ribbon Narrow gauze ribbon with black and white thin satin stripes; formerly worn as a mourning band.

Metallic or Lurex-Edged Ribbon with a narrow metallic edging, found most commonly on luxurious ribbons such as velvet or satin.

Mini Ribbon Very fine ribbon in widths from 1.5–5mm ($1/16$–$3/16$ inch), particularly suitable for delicate work such as ribbon embroidery or edging lingerie. This ribbon may be plain, mini dots, jacquard or grosgrain.

Moiré Taffeta Ribbon With a pattern which looks like a water mark, use this for making cummerbunds.

Novelty Ribbons These ribbons are often made for children and may be printed with a nursery or cartoon design. Numbers, letters of the alphabet and childrens' names are also popular, and these ribbons are sometimes used as colourful shoe laces.

Picot-Edge Taffeta Ribbon With a looped edge, the loops on these ribbons are slightly larger than on a feather-edge.

Plaid or Check Ribbon With a gingham, tartan or plaid pattern. May be made from polyester or nylon. The design may be woven in or printed onto the ribbon.

100 per cent Polyester Machine washable and dryable, these ribbons may be dry cleaned, do not need ironing and are colourfast, and are therefore particularly suitable for appliqué projects.

Satin Ribbon A shiny surfaced ribbon. Single-faced is shiny on one side, double-faced is shiny on both.

Scalloped-Edge Ribbon With a wavy edge.

Velvet Ribbon A ribbon with a soft pile or nap, it comes as a flat ribbon or in tube form; it looks good in rich colours.

Sewing Ribbons

1. Always mark the sewing line with either a marking pen or a line of tacking. Some ribbon such as satin is marked permanently by a needle and either needs to be tacked near to the edge or stuck into position using a fabric adhesive.

2. When sewing ribbon on with a machine, pin the ribbon into position. Place the pins across the width of the ribbon so that the presser foot on your sewing machine can pass over the pins easily without catching on the pin heads.

3. Always sew both edges of the ribbon in the same direction, either from top to bottom or the other way. As long as you are consistent, the ribbon will not pull. If you are sewing three or four lines of ribbon sew them in the same direction.

4. If you have a twin-needle attachment on your sewing machine, adjust it so that it is slightly narrower than the ribbon you are about to sew, and machine down both edges at the same time.

5. When sewing velvet ribbon use the zipper foot to avoid crushing the pile.

6. If you have embroidery stitches on your machine, sew a line of these down the centre of the ribbon.

7. If you have a large number of ribbons to sew next to one another, iron them onto adhesive webbing before you sew them to stop them moving about.

Gathering Ribbons

1. To make a frilled edge, sew a line of running stitches along one edge. Pull to form a gather.

2. To gather a ribbon along both edges, sew down the centre of the ribbon. First fold the ribbon in half lengthways, then sew a line of running stitches down the fold line. Pull to form gathers.

3. Shell gathering is a very pretty way of gathering stitches, and produces an edge rather like flat shells. The ribbon is marked with zig-zag creases along its length.

To mark the zig-zags, fold the right-hand end of the ribbon so that the selvage is lying across the rest of the ribbon at right angles. Make a crease on the fold. Now fold the end in the opposite direction so that the second fold runs at right angles to the first, and make another crease. Make the third fold as for the first, and continue to the end. Sew a line of running stitches along all these creases, zig-zagging up and down across the width of the ribbon. Adjust the fullness evenly when you gather up the thread.

shell gathering

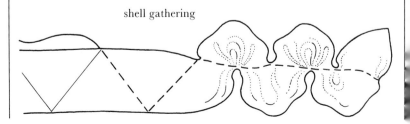

Ribbon Plaiting

Ribbon is often used for tying hair braids, but may also be used for making braids or plaits of ribbon which can be used in various ways.

Use ribbons of the same width and weight so that the braid will be even. To start, pin 3 pieces of ribbon together. If you are using long pieces of ribbon, roll each piece round a piece of card to stop them knotting.

To plait, first bring the left-hand ribbon over the centre ribbon. Then bring the right hand ribbon over the left hand ribbon which has now become the centre ribbon. Repeat. As the work grows it will become difficult to control. Either get a friend to hold the top end, or put a weight on it, so that you have something to pull against. Finish by sewing the ends together.

In the past, braiding was used for making rag rugs. The braids were coiled round and round then sewn to one another. This is not a suitable use for ribbons as they are too fine. However the coiling method may be applied to making place mats. Use the ribbons on their own or sew a backing onto the finished coil.

Plaits of narrow satin ribbon look good on satin evening bags, or evening dresses where a fine strap is required.

Make a plait of ribbon to wear as a belt – leave both ends free.

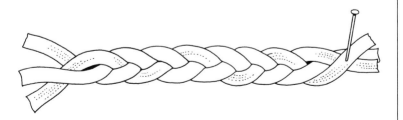

Ribbon Embroidery

Ribbons can be used in embroidery, either sewn in stitches as in slotted ribbon embroidery, or used as an outline for a pattern.

Slotted Ribbon Embroidery

This uses ribbon to make embroidery stitches. The effect is bold and the stitches are simple to do. You need a large-eyed needle, such as a tapestry needle, to carry the ribbon, and you should use a slightly open-weave fabric which will allow the ribbon to pass through easily.

Use ribbon from 1.5mm (¹⁄₁₆ inch) up to 6mm (¼ inch) in width. Anything bolder than this will look clumsy. Always start at the back of the fabric and finish at the back. Do not make your stitches too large or the ribbon will catch onto things and pucker and loop. Most embroidery stitches such as cross-stitch, herring-bone and up-and-down stitch can be done with ribbons. Look these stitches up in any book on embroidery.

Use soft ribbons for creating designs of flowers, butterflies, leaves and other natural forms. These designs may be fairly

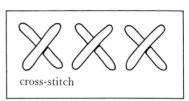
cross-stitch

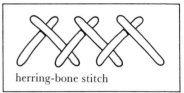
herring-bone stitch

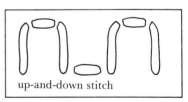
up-and-down stitch

dense and carry a large weight of ribbon, so it is a good idea to line the fabric on which you are working afterwards.

Ribbon Flower 1
1. Draw a circle on your fabric using tailor's chalk or a soft

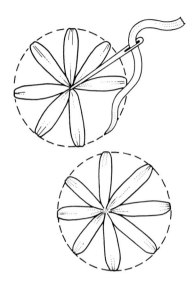

Ribbon Flower 2

*15cm (6 inches) of 19mm (¾ inch)
   ribbon*
a few sequins or small beads

1. Sew the two short sides together with a line of running stitches.
2. Along one long side, sew a row of running stitches and then gather up tightly.
3. Stitch the ribbon into position by its centre, and add either the beads or sequins to finish.

pencil. Mark the centre of the circle with a dot.
2. Bring the needle threaded with the chosen ribbon up from the underside of the fabric to the edge of the circle.
3. Put the needle back in the fabric at the dot in the centre.
4. Repeat steps 2 and 3 until the circle is complete.
5. If you wish to make a naturalistic-looking flower, instead of a formal one, make the dot to one side of the circle, and sew a combination of long and short stitches.

These flowers may be sewn by themselves, at random or in bunches. Change the colour and size according to personal taste.

Ribbon Flower 3

This third kind of embroidered ribbon flower is made by looping lengths of ribbon and catching them at their centres with either a few stitches or some small beads.

Ribbon Leaf

1. Sew 2 stitches for each leaf as in the diagram.

Outline Ribbon Embroidery

Outline embroidery is made by using narrow ribbon and sewing a line of running stitches down the centre of the ribbon. The ribbon is laid out in the pattern required and stitched into position.

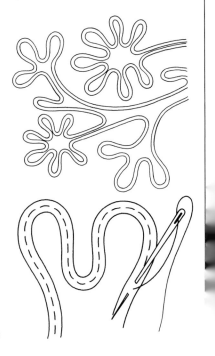

2. Use a stem stitch made from embroidery thread to make the stem, and make smaller leaves with a single ribbon stitch. Make sure you do not pull the ribbon too tightly as it looks unnatural.

Ribbon Patchwork

Patchwork is a popular craft in many countries. What started out as a thrifty way of using up scraps of cloth has developed into a highly skilled art. The early American settlers produced very beautiful patchwork quilts, many of which can still be seen today. The American Museum in Bath has some fine examples.

Narrow ribbon with woven edges lends itself to many traditional patchwork designs. Start with small projects such as cushion covers before attempting anything as large as a quilt. Each design is made up of blocks, which are then sewn together, sometimes with a border, sometimes without.

General Instructions

1. If you are mixing ribbons, make sure they are of the same weight and are dye-fast and pre-shrunk. Make sure you have plenty of contrast: mix colours, tones, stripes, spots, florals and checks.

2. Before starting your project, you need to calculate the amount of fabric required. To do this, draw the whole of the block pattern onto graph paper, the same size as the finished piece of patchwork, so that all the edges and angles are correct. (The 'block' is made up of a number of shapes which, when sewn together, form a square). One square could be used to form a cushion cover; a quilt is made up of many squares. (See the diagram on the next page.)

Colour the paper patches as if they were ribbon. Cut out each paper shape, place each colour next to the same colour, and this will show you exactly how much ribbon you require. Multiply by the number of squares if you are more ambitious and making something larger.

3. To make the pattern pieces, cut each shape out of graph paper and stick onto stiff card. Add a 6mm (¼ inch) seam allowance to all the sides and cut the card using a sharp stencil knife.

4. To machine patchwork shapes together, pin the patches together and machine using a 6mm (¼ inch) seam allowance (see diagram). Press the seams flat.

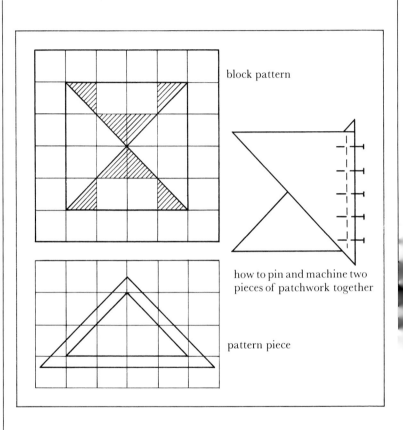

block pattern

how to pin and machine two
pieces of patchwork together

pattern piece

Here are a few traditional patterns which are suitable for ribbon
patchwork:

Stepping stones	Lady of the lake	Courthouse steps
Missouri puzzle	Cactus basket	Evening star
Devil's claw	Goose tracks	Square star
Indian trail	Pineapple	T blocks
Railroad	Log cabin	

Look in books on patchwork for all these and other designs. *Patchwork* by Avril Colby (Batsford, 1958) is a good practical patchwork instruction and history book.

Courthouse steps and log cabin, which are both made up of long thin strips, are two of the best designs for using ribbon.

Courthouse Steps

Use ribbon of equal widths and join them together in the sequence shown in the diagram.

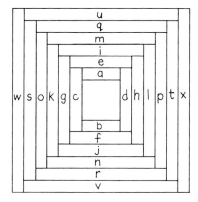

Log Cabin

This pattern is also known as barn-raising or straight furrow. The patches in log cabin are measured strips of fabric or ribbon which are sorted into light and dark shades of colour and the pattern depends on the effect made by the order of their arrangement.

1. Cut a square of backing fabric – calico is ideal. Cushions are usually made up of 15cm (6 inch) squares, quilts from 30cm–38cm (12–15 inch) squares.

2. Using a biro and a ruler, mark out the design on the backing fabric.

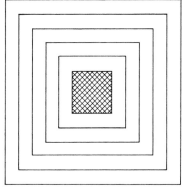

3. Tack a square of ribbon in the centre of the square.

4. The first ribbon is attached to the centre square.

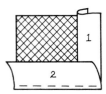

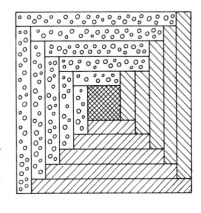

5. The second strip is sewn over the folded end of the first.
6. Repeat steps 4 and 5 until the whole of the square has been covered.

Ribbon Appliqué

Appliqué is the sewing of small pieces of fabric and/or trimmings onto larger pieces of fabric. It can be used to decorate a plain surface or to embellish an already decorated one.

Over the centuries this has been a popular craft in many cultures from the Indian deltas to the plains of North America. Appliqué can take many forms from the addition of one or two motifs, to large geometric patterns.

Ribbon particularly lends itself to appliqué work, especially if you want to make bold geometric patterns or work appliquéd letters. It has already-neatened edges and therefore can be applied with a running stitch, instead of the time-consuming close zig-zag or satin stitch needed for applying fabric with raw edges. Another method of fixing is to use 'Bondaweb', a glue-impregnated sheet made by Vilene used for bonding one fabric to another. This can be used as a sole backing sheet, or for holding ribbon into place whilst sewing onto a piece of backing fabric.

Tips

1. For appliqué to lie flat, the grain of the ribbon or fabric to be applied should run in the same direction as the base fabric.

2. Always iron both the background fabric and the ribbons before starting work.

3. When working on small areas of cloth, use an embroidery frame to hold the fabric taut whilst working the design.

4. Ribbons can be applied in gentle curves by first gathering the top edge of the ribbon and then hand hemming this edge to the background. The bottom edge of the ribbon is sewn in the normal way.

5. Appliquéd ribbon can be used to make mock bib or yoke effects on clothes.

6. Ribbon appliqué is difficult to work over a large area, so make a large item such as a quilt out of several small panels.

7. Use ribbon to cover angular pieces of fabric with frayed edges (see photograph of Mondrian-inspired cushion cover opposite page 25).

Ribbon Weaving

There are two basic types of ribbon weaving, the most common of which shows both the warp and the weft, as on the cover of this book. Look at the cushion covers from flat ribbon weaving in the photograph opposite page 25.

Flat Ribbon Weaving

This involves using ribbon both for the warp (up and down) threads and the weft (side to side). The warp and weft threads are of equal importance in the design and by clever use of ribbon you can produce interesting 3-D effects.

Before you start weaving, place ribbons next to one another to see how they look. Try unusual combinations of spots and tartans, or stripes and plains. If you are going to choose a mixture of patterns use one colour to pull the design together.

Make sure you choose ribbons that will wash if the item you are weaving is going to be in constant use.

Work out the amount of ribbon you require by drawing a life-sized pattern of the piece if a small item such as a cushion cover. For a large item such as a quilt, work out the quantity of ribbon to cover one square, and multiply by the number of squares needed to complete. Now draw each piece of ribbon next to one another, both up and down, making sure the width of each piece is accurate. Add up the number of pieces of ribbon and multiply by the length of the pattern to find the amount of ribbon required.

Basic Flat Ribbon Weaving

One of the easiest methods of ribbon weaving is to use iron-on Vilene as a base.

ribbon
iron-on Vilene
pins

1. Cut a piece of iron-on Vilene slightly bigger than the final project (this is to allow for seam allowance).
2. Place the Vilene on an ironing board with the glue side facing up.
3. Pin the warp ribbons on top of the Vilene in rows touching each other.
4. Weave the first weft ribbon under the first warp ribbon over the second, under the third etc., to the end. Pin both ends in position.
5. Weave the second ribbon over

the first ribbon and under the second etc., to the end.

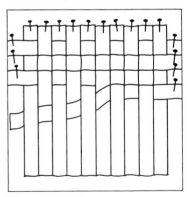

6. Repeat steps 4 and 5 until the work is complete and the Vilene is covered.
7. Cover the ribbons with a damp cloth and iron the ribbons onto the Vilene so that they fuse.
8. Remove the pins and use the fabric you have made.

Weft-Faced Ribbon Weaving

Use warp threads of cotton or linen and cover them with a ribbon weft which is pushed down to create a tightly woven fabric. This sort of weaving is normally associated with yarn rather than ribbons. However, a very interesting wall hanging or cushion cover may be woven this way.

Basic Weft-Faced Ribbon Weaving

a frame on which to weave (use either canvas stretchers or an old picture frame)
large-headed tacks
cotton or linen for the warp thread (buy this in balls from wool shops or haberdashery departments)
thick card (see method)
ribbons

1. Make the frame or loom by hammering the tacks in along the top and bottom of the loom in a zig-zag fashion, each 1.25cm (½ inch) apart.
2. Tie the cotton or linen thread to the first tack. Take it down to the first bottom tack, wind it round, and then up again to the first top tack. This is to make a strong selvage.
3. Make the rest of the warp by taking the thread up and down the frame and winding it around each tack in turn. Finish with a selvage as in step 2. Keep the thread taut at all times.
4. Make a shuttle to carry the ribbon between the warp threads from a piece of thick card 15 × 4cm (6 × 1½ inches). Cut a 4cm (1½ inch) sideways V in either end and wind ribbon around it.
5. To weave, start from the left and thread the ribbon onto the shuttle under and over the warp threads. Leave a 6cm (2¼ inch) tail of ribbon at the beginning and weave in with the next row.
6. The second row is from right to left and you go under and over the opposite threads to the first row. Be careful not to pull the ribbon too tight or the weaving will form a waist.
7. Push each row of ribbon down hard so that a dense cloth is formed.
8. Finish with two or three rows of thread to hold the ribbon in place.
9. Cut the weaving off the loom and either picture-mount it to form the front of a cushion cover,

or bind with a strong ribbon such as grosgrain.

VARIATIONS
If you are making a wall hanging why not make lots of different kinds of panel?
1. Make a shag pile by weaving short lengths of ribbon and leaving the ends loose, rather than weaving them in.
2. Weave different colour combinations. For example use black as the main colour with dashes of primary-coloured ribbon throughout.
3. Incorporate objects such as beads, feathers, shells or even bows into the weaving.

Ribbon Bows

Bows are always associated with ribbons, and it's very useful to learn how to make them properly.

Single Bow
The size of your finished bow will depend on the width of your ribbon so choose narrow ribbon for a small bow and wide for a fuller one. See the tartan bow opposite page 24.

1. Cut two pieces of ribbon: one 12.5cm (5 inches) long and the other 5cm (2 inches) long.
2. Fold the larger ribbon in half lengthways with right side facing, and sew the two ends together. Repeat with the smaller ribbon.
3. Turn them the right way round so that the seam line is in the middle centre.

4. Wrap the smaller piece of ribbon round the middle of the longer piece so that the seam is covered. Secure with a few stitches.

Shoe Bow
Sew the bent section of a clip-on earring base onto the fabric back of the bow, and then the flat part of the earring will lie against the foot.

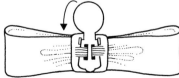

Double Bow

Make as for the single bow but use two 12.5cm (5 inch) pieces of ribbon instead of one. Lay one section on top of the other before sewing on the 5cm (2 inch) piece (see hair comb in the photograph opposite page 24).

Rosette

1. Cut four 12.5cm (5 inch) pieces and one 2.5cm (1 inch) piece of ribbon.
2. Sew each large piece as for making the single bow.
3. Make two 'crosses' by sewing one piece on top of another.
4. Turn one cross 45 degrees to make an X and one to make a +, and sew one on top of the other to make a rosette.
5. Turn the edges of the small piece of ribbon under and sew into the centre top of the rosette (see petticoat opposite page 24).

Large Gathered Bow

1. Cut three different lengths from a 19mm (¾ inch) ribbon: 20cm (8 inches); 12.5cm (5 inches); and 4cm (1½ inches).
2. With right sides facing, fold the largest piece of ribbon in half and sew up the short sides. Turn right side out.

3. Cut a sideways 'V' shape at either end of the 12.5cm (5 inch) piece of ribbon.
4. Place the sewn 20cm (8 inch) ribbon in the centre of the shaped 12.5cm (5 inch) ribbon and sew them together with running stitches up the centre of the width.
5. Gather up the running stitches, and sew the small piece of ribbon over the centre, securing it at the back. Finish in the same way as the other bows. Look at the smart blue and red bow in the photograph opposite page 24.

Flat-Tailored Bow

Wide ribbon is best for a flat-tailored bow. Use 39mm–57mm (1½–2¼ inch) wide ribbon.

1. Cut a piece of ribbon three times the desired finished width of the ribbon plus 5cm (2 inches).
2. Cut the ends diagonally. Fold the ribbon in half lengthways with right side facing and sew together across the *width* of the ribbon with a line of running stitches just under half-way from the diagonal ends, making a loop of ribbon with two ends.
3. Bring the seam to the centre of

the loop, and sew widthwise across the middle of the bow. Press open.

4. Cut a 5cm (2 inch) piece of ribbon to sew across the centre. Turn the edges in, wrap it round the bow, and sew it onto the bow at the back.

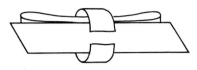

Ribbon Flowers

The most versatile flower to make out of ribbon is the rose, but violets can also be made. You can see a few ribbon flowers in the photographs. They take a little practice, but do persevere, as the end result is well worth the time spent on them.

The Rose

Polyester satin makes the most authentic looking roses. You can sew them together or wind florists' wire round to hold them together. Join them onto stems to make a bouquet or bind them together to make a bride's tiara, or to wrap around a hair comb. Sew them together for shoes, hats and clothes.

Single-faced satin is easy to work with as it doesn't slip too much, but double-faced gives a nicer finish. The size of the finished rose depends on the width of the ribbon used. Most roses are made from 12mm (½ inch), 15mm (⅝ inch), 23mm (⅞ inch), and 39mm (1½ inches) widths of ribbon. Each rose will take between 45–55cm (18–22 inches) depending on the size and fullness of bloom required.

Opposite *Bows, bags and trimmings;* Overleaf *Ribbons for baby, and for toys and fancy dress;* Facing page 25 *Ribbons for the home.*

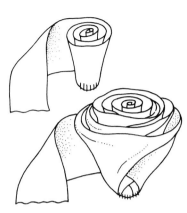

with a diagonal fold of ribbon but instead of sewing the petals into place you bind the wire tightly round after each turn. The last four items needed below are available from good florists' shops or floral supplies shops.

55cm (22 inches) ribbon
stem wires
binding wire
stem or floral tape
artificial rose leaves

Ribbon Rose

1. Cut a piece of ribbon of any of the suggested widths, and 55cm (22 inches) long.

2. Roll one end of the ribbon six times and secure it at the base with a few stitches.

3. To form petals, fold the top edge of the unwound ribbon down and towards you so that the folded edge is at 45 degrees to the rolled tube.

4. Roll the tube across the fold, and roll and tack, shaping the rose as you work.

5. Turn the raw edge under to finish.

Ribbon Rose on a Stem

Making a rose on a stem is basically the same as making a sewn rose. The petals are made

1. Make a loop about 2.5cm (1 inch) from the end of the stem wire. Fasten the binding wire to the loop by winding round and round it.

2. Cover the loop and wire with ribbon, then bind the ribbon round the covered loop six times. Now continue as for the rose.

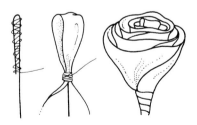

3. To finish off, cover from the base of the rose and down the stem with stem tape, adding rose leaves to the stem as you bind.

Ribbon Rose Buds

1. Make a loop on a stem, as for the stemmed rose.

2. Cut a square of ribbon and fold it in half diagonally.

3. Push the wire loop up into the fold, bring the two sides of ribbon down, and bind all the edges to the stem. Cover with stem tape.

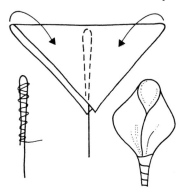

Ribbon Violets

15mm (⅝ inch) mauve ribbon
1.5mm (¹/₁₆ inch) yellow ribbon

1. Cut a 15cm (6 inch) length of mauve ribbon and a 15cm (6 inch) piece of yellow ribbon.

2. Cut the ends of the mauve ribbon into a diagonal shape.

3. Fold the ribbon into an S shape and bind in the middle with the yellow ribbon to make the first set of petals.

4. Cut another piece of mauve ribbon, fold this in an S shape and lie it on top of the first petals at right angles so it forms a cross. Bind this cross onto the first.

Use the violets to surround candlesticks, pinning them into the candle itself, and as table decorations etc.

Ribbons on Clothes

With so many kinds of ribbons available, the uses to which they can be put is almost without limit. They are especially good for transforming an old piece of clothing into something new and exciting.

Ring the Changes

Add length to a skirt by adding on some more fabric in a contrasting fabric. Use ribbon to cover the seamline at the join.

Turn a full, layered or circular skirt into a gypsy skirt by sewing rows of fine brightly coloured ribbon near to the hem of the skirt, or appliqué bands of jacquard woven ribbon with the same design, but in different colourways as in the photograph opposite page 24. Appliqué the same colour ribbons onto a piece of toning fabric for a belt, and leave long lengths of ribbon at either end of the fabric to tie in the centre and cascade from the waist.

Smarten a suit, turning a pair of black tailored trousers and jacket into the equivalent of a man's dinner suit, by sewing a line of satin ribbon, approximately 19mm (¾ inch) wide, down the outside seams of the trouser legs. You will probably have to sew the ribbon on by hand, using small neat running stitches.

Add satin or velvet ribbon to the collar and cuffs of the jacket or an old blazer.

Achieve a *trompe l'oeil* 'matelot' effect by sewing fine lines of navy blue ribbon on a plain white T-shirt, and finishing with a bow. Reverse the colour combination if you like.

Create a Coco Chanel look by adding fine black ribbon or braid 1.25cm (½ inch) in from the edge of a collarless suit.

Completely cover a garment, such as a waistcoat, in vertical strips of ribbon. There are wonderful jacquard woven ribbons which are ideal for this purpose. Use ones containing metallic thread for a dandy evening waistcoat. Something slightly more subtle, perhaps using east European motifs, is probably more suitable for daytime wear.

Make bows and attach safety pins to the back of them. Dress up clothes by pinning these bows onto necklines of dresses, to waists, and to the top of inverted pleats. Make very large ones to use as bustles, which are all the rage at the moment.

Lingerie

Transform an existing cotton broderie-anglaise petticoat or camisole by threading ribbon through the holes (see photograph opposite page 24).

Look in thrift or antique shops for old camisoles, petticoats and bloomers. These may have yellowed with age, and will probably need a good wash and maybe some bleaching to restore them to their original colour. Add ribbon in a strong contrasting colour such as red or royal blue. Wear petticoats such as these in the summer as pretty, light skirts or dresses.

Make a pretty waist slip from plain cotton and broderie-anglaise trim. Measure from your waist to your knee and multiply by two for the amount of fabric. To calculate the amount of the broderie-anglaise trim, multiply the width of the fabric by four. You will then need the same amount of narrow satin ribbon to thread through the broderie-anglaise, plus enough extra to tie a pretty bow. You will also need elastic to go round your waist.

Decorate silk lingerie with very narrow ribbon. Offray make a 1.5mm (1/16 inch) satin ribbon which is ideal for using as edging or for making little ribbon flowers, or for using to embroider initials.

If your lingerie is a pale shade such as apricot, mushroom or pink, use a toning ribbon or a variety of toning ribbons. If the garment to be embellished is black use a strong, sexy contrasting colour such as red or white.

Sweaters

Ribbons can be used to achieve very interesting effects on all sorts of woollen garments.

Thread narrow ribbon in rows through open-work sweaters.

Add a very large bow at the V of a V-necked sweater. Make it in a contrasting colour. Try exciting combinations such as tangerine on shocking pink, or acid green on lemon yellow. Sew a large black satin or velvet bow on a white fluffy angora sweater.

Edge the cuffs and neck of a sweater with pleated satin ribbon. Pleat 23mm (7/8 inch) ribbon, sew into place and then cover the join between the ribbon and the sweater with 7mm (¼ inch) ribbon.

Make an appliquéd motif using a combination of satin and ribbon. Try red satin strawberries with little green bows tied at the tops to indicate leaves; a pineapple with the segments delineated with fine ribbon; purple grapes with the leaves and stem in fine green ribbon; and butterflies or flowers.

Appliquéd Motif on a Sweater

1 sweater or sweater dress
stitch-and-tear interfacing (made by Vilene)
small pieces of wadding for interfacing
small pieces of satin in the appropriate colours
satin ribbon

1. Draw out the design on paper and make a pattern.
2. Cut shapes out of the satin.
3. Using a close zig-zag setting on a sewing machine, sew the shapes onto the interfacing.
4. Tear away the surplus interfacing and you have a complete motif.
5. If you wish to create a 3-D effect, slit the interfacing at the back of the motif and fill it with wadding, then oversew shut.
6. Stitch the ribbons and motifs on by hand. Remove them before washing.

Ribbons on Accessories

Here you can let your imagination run riot – think of shoes, belts, hats, your hair . . .

Shoes

Replace the laces in boots and shoes with beautiful coloured ribbons.

Make tiny bows from narrow ribbon and cover a pair of ballet pumps with them or sew them on to plimsolls.

Cover the toes of a pair of espadrilles in ribbons arranged to produce a rainbow effect; or outline the edges with rainbow ribbon, finishing off with a looped bow (see photograph opposite page 24).

Make shoe decorations from ribbon which are attached by clip-on earring bases. They are very easy to make and are a fraction of the price they would cost in shops. Clip-on bows may be attached to the front or back of shoes and are a real asset to someone with a limited budget and a limited wardrobe. They can be changed according to the occasion, and used as a way of matching shoes to other accessories. For how to make these bows, see pages 22–23.

Belts

Interesting belts are a cheap way of giving new life to an old outfit. For instance, you could add interest to an old leather belt by sticking a tapestry-design ribbon down its centre. Soft ribbon sewn onto a stiff interfacing is an easy way of actually making a belt, or use grosgrain on its own and fasten with a buckle. Look for old nurses' buckles in antique shops: these are usually made of very ornate silver, and were traditionally worn with a 'petersham' grosgrain belt.

Sew on top of one another two pieces of 57mm (2¼ inch) wide satin ribbon which are long enough to go round your waist, and tie up. Use two different colours for a reversible belt. Sew on lines of evenly spaced top stitching: this will give strength as well as making the belt look good.

Knitted Belt

Use one colour or try using two or three shades of the same colour. Divide the 60m (66 yards) equally between the number of colours you wish to knit. Thus for two colours – 30m (33 yards) of each, for three colours – 20m (22 yards) of each. The following ingredients and measurements are what is needed to make a belt approximately 5cm (2 inches) wide.

60m (66 yards) of 3mm (⅛ inch) wide ribbon
4½mm knitting needles
a buckle

1. Cast on 14 stitches.
2. Knit 2 rows.
3. Purl 2 rows.
4. Repeat until the work fits you around the waist plus 7.5cm (3 inches) for overlap and seam allowances. Cast off.
5. Sew the buckle onto one end of the belt.

Cummerbunds

A shaped cummerbund could be made as in the photograph opposite page 24. Decorate it by appliquéing with bands of narrow velvet ribbon edged in gold.

Another cummerbund could be made from wide velvet or satin ribbon. If the ribbon is too narrow, overlap pieces on top of one another onto a piece of interfacing to the correct width. When the interfacing is covered, sew the ribbon into place.

Hats

Ribbon may be used to enhance any sort of hat. Dress up a simple black beret by sewing a band of black satin ribbon to its edge. For evening, add a large single stone, diamanté brooch.

Ribbons are traditionally worn on straw hats, and this is an opportunity to coordinate your hat and outfit without spending much money. Change the kind of ribbon on your hat to give a new texture as well as new colour. For example change your ribbon from a shiny, soft satin ribbon to a crisper grosgrain or the soft matt pile of a velvet.

A pretty touch is to turn a straw hat into a bonnet by sewing wide satin ribbons to the underside of the hat to tie under the chin.

Make a sophisticated hat band by using two or more ribbons and twisting them together.

An interesting variation to a formal bridal head-dress and veil is a 'Juliet' cap. Make one using a stiff buckram hat base (available in most haberdashery departments), some satin fabric and lots of very narrow ribbon. Cover the hat shape with the satin. Plait the ribbons and sew around the edge of the cap. Allow strands or tendrils to hang down from the back of the cap. Alternatively, make tiny ribbon rose buds and sew these to the edge of the cap.

Ribbons in Your Hair

Ribbons have been used for dressing hair from as early as the fifteenth century. They were at their most opulent in the nineteenth century when clothes, shoes and all accessories were highly decorated with ribbons.

To make a flapper-girl head-band measure the circumference of your head and add a 2.5cm (1 inch) seam allowance. Cut a piece of ribbon this length, turn with right sides together and sew the two ends together.

To make a more substantial band, sew the ribbon onto a petersham band, or wrap the ribbon over and over the band.

Decorate a plastic Alice band by binding it tightly with narrow ribbon, using spots of glue at random intervals to secure it in place. Or make a large bow and sew it onto the Alice band.

Hair combs may be used in the same way as shoe bows to add contrast or coordination to an outfit. Use any of the bows given for shoes (pages 29–30) but sew onto combs instead of earring clips (see double bow on comb in the photograph opposite page 24).

Make ribbon ringlets. Wind narrow ribbon around a pencil, secure it into place with a pin and spray with hair spray or starch. Leave it until dry and then unwind the ringlets. Attach them in bunches to a comb.

Plait your hair with ribbon. Tie a ribbon onto the hair and substitute it for one of the bunches of hair when you make your plait; tie a ribbon at the top as well as at the bottom of a plait; or pull your hair into a bunch, then twist ribbon round the hair and roll it up into a bun.

Twist a headscarf into a 'rope' then bind it with ribbon in a criss-crossing manner. Wear it like an Alice band or a head-band.

Improvise hair slides by threading tiny bows onto hair grips.

Ribbons for Baby

You can use ribbons in a variety of ways for a baby: here are a few ideas. Look, too, at the photograph between pages 24 and 25.

Birth Quilt

75cm (30 inch) square of washable top fabric
75 cm (30 inch) square of lining fabric
75 cm (30 inch) square of 200–250g (7–8 oz) wadding
narrow ribbon

1. Using narrow ribbon (see page 12), embroider the baby's name, weight and date of birth onto the right side of the top fabric.
2. Sew the wadding onto the wrong side of the top fabric around the edges.
3. With right sides facing sew the lining fabric onto the top fabric, leaving a gap to turn through.
4. Turn right way round and close the gap by oversewing.
5. Finish with a line of topstitching around the edge, or a border of ribbons.

VARIATIONS
Instead of the name, weave cream, pale pink or pale blue ribbons as a centre panel, and finish with a ribbon border.

Sew an appliquéd panel with nursery motifs into the centre of a quilt, and finish with a ribbon border.

Sweet Things
When a baby is born to a French family, the parents give gifts of sugared almonds to their friends. Make little bags from fine cotton, fill with sugared almonds and tie with a blue or pink ribbon.

Christening Robe
Make your own christening robe from a pattern or buy a fairly plain one or a child's Victorian petticoat. Decorate them with narrow pastel-coloured ribbons as in the photograph. Decorate further with embroidery, appliqué and tiny bows as well, if you like.

Christening Cushion
Christening cushions were given as presents in Victorian times. They are small, pretty and certainly not to be played with by

children! The designs were traditionally made up of pins and old lace – the pins being used to write the name of the baby and its birthday. This version uses ribbon and pins.

2 pieces of fabric, each 12.5 × 15cm (5 × 6 inches) (choose a pale coloured silk, satin or fine cotton)
2 pieces of closely woven lining fabric, each 12.5 × 15cm (5 × 6 inches)
sawdust or bran for filling
fine ribbon in soft colours
tissue paper
rust-proof large-headed pins
grid or graph paper

1. Design the cushion on grid paper, in the same way as you would work out a cross-stitch pattern, with each square being equal to one pin head.
2. Using a soft pencil, trace the design onto the tissue paper.
3. With wrong sides facing, sew the two pieces of lining fabric together around 3½ sides.
4. Turn the right way round and fill with stuffing.
5. Close the gap by oversewing.
6. Sew the ribbon as a border around the top front piece of fabric, a little in from the edge.
7. Make little bows or rosebuds

from the same colour or contrasting ribbon for the cushion corners.
8. Make the cushion cover. With right sides together, sew the front to the back of the top fabric around three sides. Slip the cushion pad inside the cover and close the gap by oversewing.
9. Place the tissue paper on the cushion and 'pin through' the design.
10. Remove the tissue paper. This is a fiddly, time-consuming job and you may find some of the pins come out. If this happens, simply replace them. Push all the pins well down.
11. If you are also using lace or broderie-anglaise sew this on by hand.
12. Sew the bows or ribbons onto the corners.

Baby's Changing Bag/Mat

A useful present for a new baby is a baby changing bag-cum-mat. This is a bag for carrying all the baby's belongings, which also becomes a nappy-changing surface. Offray make some wonderful, brightly coloured grosgrain ribbons which are perfect for making the shoulder straps and binding.

45 × 75cm (18 × 30 inches) piece of
brightly coloured outer fabric in
canvas gabardine or similar
45 × 75cm (18 × 30 inches) piece of
towelling or PVC for lining
(towelling is machine washable;
PVC can be wiped down after
accidents but has to be hand
washed)
45 × 75cm (18 × 30 inches) of 250g
(8 oz) wadding
3.6m (4 yards) of 23mm (⅞ inch)
grosgrain ribbon for binding
2.75m (3 yards) of 39mm (1½ inch)
grosgrain ribbon for the straps
1.2m (1⅓ yards) of poppers on a tape

1. Fold the outer fabric in half
crossways and mark the half-way
point with a line of pins.
2. Stitch the ends of the 39mm
(1½ inch) ribbon together, then
place it on the right side of the
outside fabric as in the diagram.
Check the handles are of even
size before stitching.
3. Sew the edges of the wadding
to the wrong side of the towelling
or PVC.
4. With wrong sides facing, sew
the lining to the outer fabric
around all the sides.
5. Bind the edges with the 23mm
(⅞ inch) ribbon.

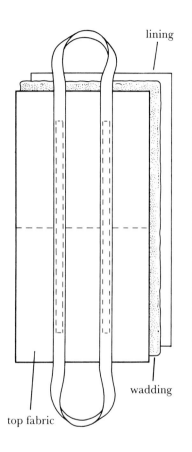

lining

wadding

top fabric

6. Sew each length of the popper
tape to just inside the bound
edges of the bag, making sure
they are aligned when the bag is
closed.

Toys Using Ribbons

Ribbons can make toys of all kinds, shapes and sizes, and can also transform dressing-up clothes. The photograph between pages 24 and 25 shows many of these items.

Play Ball

These play balls are attractive and an eye-catching present for a baby. Hang one on a piece of elastic to bounce up and down, or thread a string of them across a pram or buggy.

felt
ribbon, not wider than 12mm (½ inch)
round elastic
wadding or cotton wool (or old tights)
  for filling

1. Cut out six segments in felt, from the pattern given on the opposite page.
2. Sew the pieces together leaving a gap for the stuffing.
3. Thread the elastic through the top of the ball.
4. Fill the ball with stuffing, and oversew remaining gap.
5. Sew lines of brightly coloured ribbon down the seam lines.

Play Mat

Appliqué a miniature landscape with roads to run toy cars on and rails for trains. Use wide black ribbon for the road, with narrow yellow ribbon for the no-parking lines, and white ribbon down the centre of the road.

Games Play Mat

Appliqué a mat with traditional board games such as a draughts/chess board, snakes and ladders, ludo and, if your sewing skills are up to it, Monopoly. Ribbon is the easiest way of delineating all the separate sections of the mat.

Hobby Horse

Make a hobby horse using a simple shaped head cut out of felt, heavy-duty cotton or canvas, a broom or two pieces of dowelling, and lots of pretty ribbons.

Stuff the head with wadding and make a slit in the neck for a handle, which is tied to the pole inside the head before sewing up the bottom. Use ribbons to make his bridle, to decorate him, and to dangle down.

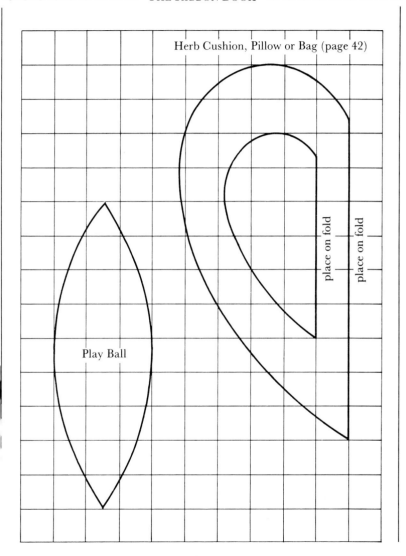

Herb Cushion, Pillow or Bag (page 42)

place on fold

place on fold

Play Ball

Paint the handle a bright colour and then wind long pieces of narrow ribbon round it.

Play Tent
Make a tent from an old sheet, which you can either hang over a washing line or tie onto an old clothes horse.

1. Fold the sheet in half so that when it hangs over a washing line it reaches the ground. Trim off any excess fabric.
2. Bind all the edges with grosgrain ribbon.
3. Draw in the windows and cut out the centre fabric from each,

leaving a 1.25cm (½ inch) seam allowance all around.
4. Snip into each corner and fold the seam allowance back. Machine into place and edge with more grosgrain ribbon.
5. Make window bars from more grosgrain ribbon; sew into place.
6. Cut a piece of ribbon the length of the tent and sew into position down the middle.
7. Sew a 2.5cm (1 inch) curtain ring to each end of the piece of ribbon.
8. Make loops for skewer tent pegs.

To make a clothes-horse tent, measure the fabric against the clothes horse and make ribbon ties at the corners. Make the windows as for the washing-line tent.

Decorate the outside of the tent with flowers, leaves and butterflies made of ribbons (see Ribbon Embroidery, page 12).

Dressing-Up Clothes

Make simple dress or tunic shapes by drawing round a T-shirt shape, then decorate with ribbons.

Jester's Outfit

Cut the bottom edges into V shapes, and decorate the T-shirt with contrasting coloured ribbons, for example yellow/blue, red/green, black/white. Sew bells onto the cut points.

Fairy's Outfit

Gather three layers of netting onto a wide satin ribbon long enough to tie at the back. Bind the edges with narrow satin ribbon. Wear this over a leotard. Make a wand from a piece of narrow dowelling wound with

narrow ribbon. Stick a star and streamers of ribbon on the top.

Indian's Outfit

Make a head-band from two pieces of ribbon. Pin real feathers between them and then sew together.

Make a tunic from a T-shirt shape with the ends fringed, and decorate with fine ribbon threaded with wooden beads.

Clown Suit

Make an all-in-one or jump-suit shape from brightly coloured remnants of fabric. Decorate with zig-zag bands of narrow, brightly coloured ribbons, as shown in the photograph.

Sew bands of gingham ribbon 7.5cm (3 inches) from the bottom of each sleeve and trouser leg. Thread these bands of ribbon with elastic to form a cuff.

Make a collar by gathering 5cm (2 inch) ribbon and attaching to the neck.

Magician's Cloak

Make a cloak from half a circle or black satin, edge it with a wide red ribbon and make wide red ribbon ties.

Rag Doll's Wardrobe

Ribbons are a must in dolls' clothes-making. They can be used as trimmings, for making accessories and for making complete outfits for small dolls.

The rag doll in the photograph has 12mm (½ inch) woven jacquard ribbon as a trim on the sleeves, across the bodice and as a trim on the hem of her skirt. The bottom of her petticoat is made up of 39mm (1½ inch) wide shocking pink grosgrain ribbon with a border of 19mm (¾ inch) floral jacquard woven ribbon and finished off with white lace.

She has a band of shocking pink grosgrain tied round her middle and tied in a big bow at the back. Her shoes are made from 39mm (1½ inch) wide shocking pink grosgrain, with straps made from 9mm (⅝ inch) grosgrain of the same colour. She has a blue polka-dot ribbon in her hair to match her eyes.

Ribbon Presents

There are a number of ideas which can be made into presents from ribbon. You can, obviously, give a cushion cover (or a quilt!), or Christening presents to new babies; here are a few more suggestions.

Rosette Earrings

1m (just over a yard) of 15mm (⅝ inch) or 19mm (¾ inch) satin ribbon

clip-on earring backs with perforated cups (these are little holes for sewing)

1. Cut the ribbon in half. Use one piece for each earring.
2. Sew a line of running stitches up the centre of the ribbon, gather the stitches up evenly and coil the ribbon round itelf. Sew the pieces of the coil together with a few running stitches.
3. Sew the ribbon coil onto the perforated ear cup, and attach the cup, by means of its clips, onto the earring back.

Earrings with Bows

Make bows and attach to earring bases, or thread on an eye pin and hang from an earring base.

Bow Tie

These are good made in satin or velvet ribbon.

enough ribbon to make a large bow (see pages 22–23)
ribbon to fit neck circumference plus 5cm (2 inches) for overlap and seam allowance
5cm (2 inches) of Velcro

1. Make bow (see pages 22–23).
2. Neaten the ends of the ribbon to go around the neck.
3. Sew the Velcro onto either end of the piece you have neatened and thread the bow onto it.
4. Secure the bow into position in the middle of the ribbon with a few stitches.

Small Shoulder Purse

See this purse in the photograph opposite page 24.

1 piece lining fabric, 11.5 × 36cm (4½ × 14 inches)
enough ribbon to cover the fabric: try interesting combinations of patterns, mixing plaids, dots and stripes, or keep it simple and sophisticated with some striped grosgrain
90cm (1 yard) of 19mm (¾ inch) wide ribbon for the binding
90cm (1 yard) of narrow ribbon for the strap
press studs

1. Cover the lining fabric with ribbon and sew into position.
2. Bind both narrow ends of the fabric with the 19mm (¾ inch) ribbon to neaten.
3. With the lining fabric on the inside, fold about one-third of the fabric up so it measures 14cm (5½ inches) from the fold at the front. Pin, then sew up the sides to form the pocket.
4. Bind the remaining raw edges with binding ribbon.
5. Sew the ends of the strap to the top of the pocket.
6. Sew one-half of a press stud to the centre wrong side of the flap and to the corresponding spot on the outside of the pocket.

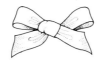

Herb Cushion, Pillow or Bag
This can be made as a small heart-shaped cushion or a herbal pillow, or as a little bag to hang on a coathanger or put in a drawer.

enough fabric for the front and back of the cushion
100g (4 oz) pot-pourri or lavender flowers
pretty ribbon pieces

1. Enlarge the larger heart pattern given on page 37.
2. Place the pattern on the fold of the fabric and cut two heart-shaped pieces.
3. Sew the ribbon in rows onto the right side of one piece of fabric to make the front of the cushion.
4. With right sides together, sew the front onto the back leaving a 5cm (2 inch) gap to turn through.
5. Cut away any excess seam allowance at the points and curves of the heart before turning it the right way out.
6. Fill with lavender or pot-pourri.
7. Close the gap by oversewing.

To make a little lavender bag use the smaller pattern and sew on a loop of ribbon from which to hang it.

Ribbons for Packaging

Wrapping presents beautifully demands no great skill or expense, and the time and effort involved can transform even the most humble present into something of great worth. Try some of the following ideas, and look at the photograph opposite page 25.

Edible Present Wrapping
If you are giving a present of a jar of home-made preserve, make a pretty fabric top tied with a piece of ribbon.

If you are giving biscuits such as macaroons, individually wrap them in white tissue paper parcels tied with narrow ribbon, and place in an attractive tin, box or small basket if you have one.

Put sweets in a glass jar (an old coffee jar with the lid given a coat of

bright paint is a good stand-by). Tie a large piece of ribbon round the middle and finish with a bow.

Baskets

Baskets wound with ribbons, with ribbons woven into them and bows tied onto them, make beautiful presents. Use them to hold presents of flowers, fruit, bath salts, talc etc. See the photograph showing things for a baby.

Gift Tags

Save old birthday and Christmas cards to cut up, punch a hole in the corner and thread with a piece of pretty ribbon. Or glue a scrap of wrapping paper onto thin white card. Fold it in half and trim to a rect-angular shape. Punch a hole in the top corner near the fold, and thread ribbon through the hole to tie onto the present.

Ribbon Pom-Poms

Instead of using ready-made ones, make your own from a reel of ribbon viscose (available in most card shops and department stores).

Twist the ribbon in figure-of-eight shapes, over and over again until you get a pom-pom shape. As the ribbon is likely to untie as you work use Blue-tak to stick each centre onto the previous one, and then use Blue-tak to stick the pom-pom onto the parcel.

Ribbon Ringlets

Stretch a piece of viscose ribbon over the closed blades of a pair of scissors. Do it several times until it forms a ringlet. Make half a dozen of different lengths and hang them together from your present.

Ribbons for the Home

Ribbons can decorate bedlinen, towels, lampshades and coathangers, and be made up into pretty picture frames. Try a few of the following ideas.

Picture Frames

Buy ready-made picture frames of card from good craft shops and decorate them with a border of narrow ribbon. Or wind ribbon round and round the frame (as in the photograph opposite page 25) to cover it completely.

Coathanger 1

This first version is very quick to make.

1 coathanger, 40cm (16 inches)
5m (5½ yards) of 6mm (¼ inch)
   ribbon
fabric adhesive

1. Wind the ribbon round the coathanger as tightly as you can, dabbing glue onto the hanger as you wind.
2. Make a ribbon rose or bow (see pages 22–26), and hang it over the hook.

Coathanger 2

This second hanger is padded, and the example in the photograph opposite page 25 has narrow ribbon in a criss-cross pattern across it rather than the ribbon roses.

50cm (20 inches) of 1.25cm (½ inch)
   ribbon
20cm (8 inches) of 90cm (36 inch)
   pretty cotton fabric (choose a
   small-flower Liberty print or
   something similar)
1 wooden coathanger, 40cm (16
   inches)
20cm (8 inches) of thick polyester
   wadding
adhesive (Copydex is ideal)
enough ribbon to make 3 ribbon roses
   (page 25)

1. Glue ribbon to hook, beginning at the tip, to cover it.
2. Cut a piece of wadding the length of the coathanger and wide enough to go round it, plus 1.25cm (½ inch) all round.
3. Cut a small hole in the centre of the wadding and push the coathanger through it. Fold the wadding round the coathanger and tack it in place.
4. Cut a strip of fabric twice the

length of the padded coathanger and wide enough to go round it, plus a 2cm (¾ inch) seam allowance all round. Cut the corners to a rounded shape.

5. Snip a small hole at the centre for the hook and turn in and press all the raw edges.

6. Put the cover on the coathanger, and pin the edges together. Sew a line of small running stitches close to the edge through all thicknesses. Pull up the gathers until the cover fits the coathanger. Make sure they are spread evenly, and cast off.

7. Make ribbon roses (page 25), and hang from a piece of ribbon over the hook of the hanger.

Bed Linen

If you are on a limited budget, or have perhaps inherited some plain bed linen and wish to make something exciting from it, ribbons can be a great source of inspiration.

Rows of Narrow Ribbon

Sew evenly spaced, brightly coloured ribbons in lines as a border to a primary coloured sheet or duvet cover (see photograph opposite page 25.

Choose red and blue to go on yellow, green on red, orange and red on yellow. Make matching pillowcases. Or pick out a colour from your carpet or curtains and choose a colour to match.

Pretty Pastel Shades

Sew lines of pale coloured ribbons – cream, pink and white – as an edging to a white sheet. Use by themselves or intersperse with lace or broderie-anglaise. Edge the pillow cases in the same way.

Using Remnants

Before using remnants to make bed linen make sure they are pre-shrunk, colourfast and machine washable. Make a duvet cover from pieces of narrow width fabric sewn together. Use ribbon to cover and strengthen the seam lines. Make the underside of the duvet from an old sheet or buy plain sheeting (available in most good department shores).

Ribbon Ties for Duvets, etc

Use ribbon ties as a cheap and easy fastening. For a duvet use 30cm (12 inch) pieces of ribbon sewn to the neatened opening at

25cm (10 inch) intervals. Make sure the top and the bottom pieces of ribbon match up.

Mondrian Inspired Designs

The Dutch artist Mondrian painted pictures consisting of blocks of primary colours broken up with bold lines of black. If you like a strong bold statement, imitate these paintings to create a duvet cover. Use blue, red and white fabric squares and

rectangles sewn together with the seam lines covered in black ribbon. (See the 'Mondrian' cushion in the photograph facing page 25.)

Children's Bed Linen

Look in children's picture books for ideas which can be appliquéd in ribbon. Anything with straight sides and right angles is ideal, such as kites. The tail has real bows!

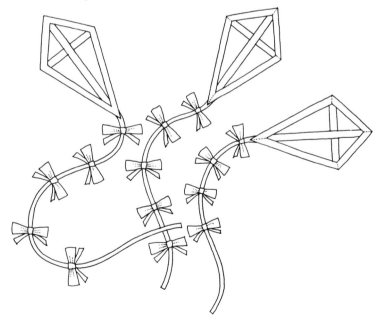

Finishing Touches

The following are a few more ribbon ideas for the home.

Ribbon Border for a Lampshade
A good way of coordinating an existing lampshade with new curtains, is to pick out one of the colours in ribbon and use it as a border.

Measure round the top and bottom of the lampshade and add 5cm (2 inches) to this measurement for seam allowances. Cut the ribbon so that it measures the same as the circumference of both the top and bottom of the shade plus 2.5cm (1 inch). First work on the top of the shade and then the bottom. Begin at the seam and apply a little glue to the edge of the shade. Stick the ribbon in place folding under 1.25cm (½ inch) at the end. Continue round to where you started. Trim the end if necessary, leaving enough ribbon to turn under 1.25cm (½ inch), then stick it in place so that the two ends match up. Do the bottom in the same way.

Towels
With the easy-care, colourfast, machine-washable ribbons now available even in satin, why not add some luxury to your bathroom.

Sew one or two lines of satin ribbons 7.5cm (3 inches) up from the bottom of either end of your towels. Use ribbon the same colour as the towel or maybe a tone darker as the contrast in the texture will look more sophisticated than a strong colour contrast.

Curtain Tie-Backs
Use wide double-faced satin ribbon for tying back bedroom curtains. Use stick-on Velcro to attach the ribbon to the wall and the centre of the ribbon. Tie the ribbon in a large bow.

Acknowledgements

The author and publishers wish to thank the following people for their generous help:

Offray Ribbons
C. M. Offray and Son Ltd, Fir Tree Place, Church Road, Ashford, Middlesex TW15 2PH.

If you have problems finding ribbon stockists, please write to Offray at the above address.

Tootal Craft

Vilene

Hobby Horse
15–17 Langton Street, London SW10 0JL.
For providing the clip-on earring bases.

Brother and Jones for the use of the 'Compal Galexie' electronic sewing machine, used to make most of the items in this book.

Dorma who supplied the sheets.

Liberty who supplied their small print cotton lawn fabric.